101 Essays to Empower You to Peak Performance

Frank Agin
Founder & President
AmSpirit Business Connections

ISBN: 978-1-967521-17-3

Published by:
418 Press, A Division of Four Eighteen Enterprises LLC
Post Office Box 30724, Columbus, Ohio 43230-0724

Acknowledgement

In sincere appreciation of Linda Agin.

Life partner.

Parenting co-captain.

Business colleague.

Workout companion.

Table of Contents

Look For These Other Books in This Series

101 Essays to Empower You to Rise & Thrive
101 Essays to Empower You to Up Your Game
101 Essays to Empower You to Build Momentum
101 Essays to Empower You to Limitless Reach
101 Essays to Empower You to Elevate Your Influence
101 Essays to Empower You to The Winning Edge
101 Essays to Empower You to Live Unstoppable
101 Essays to Empower You to Achieve Greatness
101 Essays to Empower You to Break Barriers

Introduction

This book comes from the insight and creativity of Frank Agin.

Who is Frank? He is the founder and president of AmSpirit Business Connections, an organization that empowers entrepreneurs, sales representatives, and professionals to become successful and gain more referrals through networking.

He is the author of several books, including Foundational *Networking: Building Know, Like and Trust to Create a Lifetime of Extraordinary Success* and *The Three Reasons You Don't Get Referrals*. See all his books and programs at frankagin.com.

Finally, Frank shares information and insights on professional relationships, business networking and best practices for generating referrals on the Networking Rx podcast.

In the summer of 2018, he started planning this short-form podcast. As he mapped out what he wanted to bring to an audience of entrepreneurs, sales representatives, and professionals, he knew he'd have hundreds of programs.

But in addition to all that content, Frank noticed he also had a plethora of other materials—instructive, insightful, and inspirational. All this additional content was worthwhile, but none of it was long enough to create a full episode of Networking Rx.

Not wanting the material to go to waste, Frank developed it into short essays—approximately 150 words each. Then he started to record and share those segments daily under the brand Networking Rx Minutes.

For years, he shared a daily message of empowerment, intuition, and hope. This is a compilation of 100 of those essays. Enjoy.

-1-
Root For Everyone

In his book *No One Gets There Alone*, sports psychologist Dr. Rob Bell shared that "During one game in 1995, Joe Smith of the Maryland Terrapins was unstoppable. He scored 40 points, had 18 rebounds, and had a tip-in basket as time expired to defeat the Duke Blue Devils, 94-92.

At the end of the game, the fans applauded the effort. No surprise, right? Wrong. The game was at Duke University and those cheering fans were Blue Devil faithful.

Bell uses this story to encourage you to root for everybody. He shares, "We in fact need others at their best because it is the way we make ourselves better. All historic rivalries were based on two greats performing at their best." He goes on to share examples, such as Ali/Frazier, Nicklaus/Palmer, Coke/Pepsi and Ford/GM.

In fact, he points out, you need others to succeed so you know how to improve. And this demonstrates that you are enough to actually wish the best for others.

-2-
A Healed Femur

A student once asked anthropologist Margaret Mead, "What was the earliest sign of civilization?" The student expected her to say a clay pot, a grinding stone, or maybe a weapon. Mead thought for a moment, then she said, "A healed femur."

As the longest bone in the body, it takes about six weeks of rest for a fractured femur to heal. And the healing of this bone, which connects the hip and knee, showed compassion. Someone cared for the injured person. They did their hunting and gathering. They offered protection.

Mead explained that in nature, where survival of the fittest is the rule, healed femurs are not found amongst any other species. Thus, the first sign of civilization was the compassion to see through the healing of a broken femur.

No doubt, as a unique human being, you have wonderful skills and talents. Harnessing language and utilizing technology. But what makes you best of all is the compassion hardwired in your DNA. Never pass up an opportunity to share it.

-3-
Your Networking Piggybank

Do you remember the piggy bank you had as a kid? It was difficult to open but simple to deposit occasional bits of spare change found in couches or car seats, earned from errands, or gifted by the tooth fairy.

Whatever, however, you saved a penny here. You saved a nickel or dime there. And occasionally a quarter or two. Then at some point, you had amassed a kid-sized small fortune, that you could use to acquire something of great value.

Your networking efforts work in a similar fashion. No, a networking piggy bank doesn't hold U.S. legal tender. It does, however, hold social capital, which is your ability to draw benefits from the people you're associated with.

And this social capital, like the traditional piggy bank, builds a bit here and there. It builds via each handshake, via each small conversation, via each introduction, via each encouraging word. Then one day, you can draw on that social capital to achieve things of great value.

-4-
The Most Enjoyable Path

In her book *Becoming Competition Proof: Stand Out And Overcome Competition Through Generosity, Service And Added Value*, speaker and consultant Berta Medina-Garcia shares, "The truth is, the fastest and most enjoyable path to success is in helping others succeed. The moment that you shift the focus of your business from simply making money to helping others succeed and adding value, your success is inevitable."

Berta, as everyone knows her, implies that far too often chasing money gets in the way of truly just serving others. And the failure to serve others, stands in the way of achieving the success you truly want.

So, ignore the money for a moment and focus on serving. Be a connector of great people. Be a purveyor of opportunity. And be a dealer of inspiration, a beacon of hope and a source of useful information. If you do, success and money will find you. You will have just taken the most enjoyable path to getting there.

-5-
Be a Quitter

Best-selling author and personal development specialist Lewis Howes shared on social media, "If you want to quit anything: Quit making excuses Quit lying to yourself. Quit waiting for the right time. Quit trying to be perfect. Quit trying to fit in. And start becoming the person and professional you were born to be!"

WOW! This quote can be both indicting and inspiring. If any piece of this is true of you – even a little bit in that quiet moment of self-reflection – then this quote can be a stinging realization. A realization that you have some quitting to do.

But at the same moment, Howes' words can serve as an inspiration. How? Simple. No matter how guilty you might be of making excuses, lying to yourself, waiting for the right time, or whatever, it never too late to quit.

Today. Right now. You can resolve to become the person you were born to be and in so doing commit to being a quitter.

-6-
A Confused Mind

No doubt, you are good at what you do. And part of the reason for that is that there is much to what you do. You can serve lots of different clients. And you can serve those clients in a variety of different ways. And that's great.

But while all of that is great, if you're not careful it can serve to impair you too. How? At times, those with vast educations, experiences and abilities can overcomplicate what they have to offer. They feel the need to say too much or complicate things with jargon or industry speak.

Remember, that a confused mind says "NO." Thus, keep whatever you have to say simple. Distill what you have to say down to a sentence or two that most anyone can get their head around.

If necessary, use an appropriate example or anecdote to clarify your message. You've worked hard to be able to offer all you do. So, don't lose out on opportunity because of your messaging.

-7-
Don't Try, Just Be

In her book *The 11 Laws of Likability*, speaker and personal relationship expert Michelle Tillis Lederman relates that you're at your best when you're just being your genuine self. She shares, "Authenticity is who you are – your honest reactions, your natural energy. Sharing what is real about you is the key to building real relationships with others."

Lederman goes on to imply that authenticity is the foundation upon which everyone comes to know you, like you, and eventually trust you. But moreover, she shares that who you are is the easiest persona from which to operate.

When it comes to being authentic, there is no practicing or scripting required. Who you are, just is.

When it comes to being authentic, you don't need to focus on some false pretense that you hope will win others over. Rather, you just need to relax and be yourself. When it comes to being authentic, you don't have to try, you just need to be.

-8-
The Slippery Slope

If you long to be known as the generous sort (and everyone should), then no doubt you are on the lookout for a wonderful opportunity to contribute to the world around you. The problem is that those wonderful opportunities are not at all easy to find. Generally, by the time you hear of them, someone else has already acted on the moment.

But if you're truly interested in making an impactful contribution to the world around you, stop looking and waiting for the big moments. Rather, start by simply acting on the small ones. You know, finding opportunities for smaller contributions. Agreeing to take on that not-so-glamourous role in that charitable initiative. Or stepping up to undertake that random act of kindness.

This is the reality: Generous operates on a slippery slope. Whenever you engage in a small act of altruism, you tend to slide on into the bigger opportunities.

-9-
Zero Times Anything Equals

Early on in your math days, you were taught that zero times one equals zero. Zero times ten is equal to zero. Even zero times 400-gagillion equals zero. Any number times zero comes out to zero. Simple, right?

Much like in mathematics, where zero times any other number equals zero, excellence in any aspect of our life is meaningless if there's zero reliability. A great work ethic will get you nowhere unless you do what you say. Wonderful creativity is critically handicapped if you don't honor your word.

Reliability is everything. There is no middle ground. Reliability is like a contract. You say to others, "In exchange for your trust, I will do what I say I am going to do when I say I am going to do it."

So, if someone says they can depend on you, take pride in that. And don't let them down. They've declared you reliable, which is the highest compliment of all.

-10-
Thank You Cards

In his book *MORE: Word of Mouth Referrals, Lifelong Customers and Raving Fans*, networking consultant and professional speaker Matt Ward reminds us: "Always keep a package of thank you cards in your desk. You never know when you're going to need one."

Ward goes on to share, "Giving thanks is one of the simplest ways to let your contacts know you appreciate them." He's right. And he goes on to imply that, in reality, you have lots to be thankful for and should being sending thank you notes often. Brainstorm all that you can share thanks for.

Thanks for the referral. Thanks for the introduction. Thanks for taking the time to talk to me, share with me, or encourage me. Thanks for the great service. Thanks for saying thanks.

There is no shortage of things for which you can give thanks. You simply need to take the time to offer it to others.

-11-
Currency of Success

Social media has become the game changing, groundbreaking innovation of the 21st century. It has given the tiniest voices a platform from which to be heard. It has allowed small business American to level the playing field with corporate America.

With it, you might feverishly attempt to contribute opinion and insight in the hopes of establishing influence with people you might never have met. As you do, however, remember this: While likes, comments and shares are wonderful, those digital bits of technology alone do not create success.

Sure, accumulating the validation and accolades of others has some value. But the reality is that business is done between people. And for that to happen, individuals need to establish a mutual sense of knowing, liking, and trusting one another.

So, while reactions to your posts are important, in the end what's vital are human connections. So, remember to still connect with people in a real human way. After all, relationships are the true currency of success.

-12-
Write-Review-Use-Refine

No matter who you are or what you do, you have dozens of options for sharing about yourself. So, figuratively have a handful of these options ready to pull out of your back pocket.

Like anything, however, you won't get good at delivering these without a little preparation, planning and practice. Here are some thoughts to make that happen.

1 - Write Them: Using something as basic as a small note pad or 3x5 cards, neatly write or type your commercials for future reference.

2 - Review Them: Once you have them written out, keep them handy so that you can practice or review them from time to time.

3 - Use Them: When someone then asks, "Who are you?", do not hesitate. Have the courage to share what makes the most sense for the time and place.

4 - Refine Them: These statements about you are always a work in progress. You should look for ways to regularly update them to better represent you.

-13-
Go Take a Hike

In a newsletter entitled *Positive Psychology Tools with the Biggest Bang for Your Buck,* executive coach and relationship expert Dr. John Schinnerer shared that an effective way of improving you overall happiness is to commit to spending 20 minutes a day on a walk outside your office.

Schinnerer goes on to share that when you're in nature, surrounded by trees, birds, flowers and fresh air it serves to increase your vitality. It reboots your mood. And this cannot help but improve your overall happiness. And as a bonus, this activity even boosts the functioning of your immune system.

So, the next time someone at work tells you to go take a hike, thank them. And act on that advice. It will serve to brighten your mood and put you – mind and body – in a better place.

-14-
Coaches Versus Commentators

The average salary of head coaches in major professional sports is approximately 100 times the average salary of those who offer commentary on those athletic endeavors.

Why? Simple. Society places relatively little importance on the efforts of those simply offering after-the-fact opinions on what could've or should've been in any particular game, match or contest.

And at the same time, market force recognizes the immense value provided by those who strategize in solitude, involve others in the preparation and then execute on the game plan – even though they risk great failure.

The lesson you can bring to your world is that to achieve great things you need to be more like a coach than a commentator. Don't just opine on the actions of others. Rather, formulate a wonderful vision, attempt to involve others, and then work tirelessly to execute on it. And if for whatever reason, any piece of the plan fails, ignore the critics, and keep going.

-15-
The Water and The Mountain

Every winter in the Rockies, snowfall builds and creates icy, white mountain peaks. Then in the spring, warmer temperatures cause this ice pack to melt, and the gravity pulls the water downward.

As it moves down the mountain, the water does not follow a straight path. Rather it weaves around obstacles encrusted in the mountain. The water, however, never says to the mountain, "Will you get out of my way?" Instead, the water says, "No worries. I will find a different way!" And it sets about finding a path of least resistance.

Just like the water, your journey to success will meet with obstacles. Some might have been intentionally placed there by others, perhaps to deter you. Others might just naturally occur and simply be a part of life.

Whatever the case, be like the water. Do not be dissuaded. Use your ingenuity. Become flexible in your approach. Do whatever. But simply, find another way to success.

-16-
Surviving Category 5 Events

In an interview on the Networking Rx podcast, Christine Perakis, a business growth architect, and author of *The Resilient Leader: Life-Changing Strategies to Overcome Today's Turmoil and Tomorrow Uncertainty*, shared her experiences living through two Category 5 hurricanes that struck the British Virgin Islands over consecutive weeks.

What was her advice for surviving these natural catastrophes? Hunker down? Nope! Seek higher ground? Wrong again! Flee? That is simply not an option, amid the storm or its aftermath.

Perakis' advice is to simply focus on helping others. You see, when you focus outward on others you move from your own personal (and often debilitating) fear to more rational and courageous thinking. You become more resolved. You become more creative and open to finding solutions.

While you might never find yourself in a hurricane, Category 5 like events will still hit you. Trying relationships. Career or business turmoil. Health challenges. In tumultuous times, help yourself survive by focusing on helping others.

-17-
Building Trust

Admit it, you have a natural trust for the person who does what they say they are going to do. With that, to earn the trust of others, you should become the person upon whom others can rely.

So, answer this: What other traits in people make them trustworthy in your eyes? Being diligent and conscientious? Sure! Then you should endeavor to be those, too.

Honest and fair? Absolutely! Then strive to be honorable and even-handed with everything that you do.

Open-Minded? You bet! Then guard yourself against forming opinions without all the facts in hand.

You should try to mimic these trust-building behaviors. In short, become the person you want to associate with. After all, if you endeavor to mirror the characteristics, attitudes and habits of those you aspire to cohort with, legions of others will strive to be with you – giving you much more in the end.

-18-
Just Don't Quit

More often than not, people don't fail. They don't really fail in school. They don't really fail in business. They do not really fail in relationships. More often than not, people simply stop practicing the habit of persistence. In other words, they quit.

Regarding education, they don't fail. Rather, they quit trying to learn. They don't fail, they just fail to give effort.

Businesses don't fail. The people behind them quit. They quit trying to find new clients. They quit trying to innovate to a better way of serving others. They simply stop chasing business success. It's just easier to get a J-O-B.

When it comes to relationships, there is no failure but rather an abandonment of what makes relationships work. They quit listening. Being understanding. Being open to compromise. Being empathetic.

The reality is that you can be successful at just about anything. Education. Business. Even life. Start whatever and then just don't quit.

-19-
Excuses Reveal Fears

On Twitter, corporate psychologist and motivational speaker Tim Shurr shares that, "Your biggest breakthroughs are hidden in the places you don't want to go. Identify your fears by the excuses you make for not taking action and then make solving those fears your goal. Your impediments become your path! Your blocks are also your steppingstones."

Shurr repeats his advice on his *How To Be Mesmerizing* podcasts and in his books. The gateways to your greatest moments often look like obstacles that, for a moment, you can't see a way around, over or through.

But what if, next time you're stuck in business or life, you confront the very thing that you believe to be stopping you and ask yourself, "How can I use this to my advantage?" or, "What is the opportunity in the very thing that seems to have me stymied?"

As Shurr counsels, ponder those questions and doorways will open and paths will appear.

-20-
Postcards

On his YouTube video series *Networking Superchargers*, uber-connector and social architect Pablo Gonzalez shares an insight on remaining connected as well as being impactful. He shares that whenever you travel, you should make a point of purchasing a handful of postcards. Then get those sent to people in your network.

Interesting, huh? First of all, the effort is generally quick as you don't get much room to write anyway. And it's also very inexpensive. Postcards are seldom costly and postage to mail them is downright cheap.

But the most wonderful thing about this suggestion is that it can serve to brand you as totally unique. People stay connected through electronic newsletters. At the holidays, they might send a card. And the best of the best, will craft a handwritten note.

But a postcard, now that tells someone that while I was away from the office, I saw something that made me think of you. That will get anyone's attention.

-21-
Networking Vehicle

Over the years, writers, speakers, and trainers have applied many analogies, metaphors, and similes to networking. Here is one. Networking is a vehicle, as it serves to move you from one point to another. But it's not just any vehicle. It's one with incredible versatility.

It can be a supersonic jet, flying you quickly to new heights.

It can be a wind-swept sailboat, gently and quietly gliding you along to where you want to go.

It can be that locomotive, powerfully moving you along with an almost unstoppable force.

It can be the family SUV, allowing you to take advantage of it for business or for pleasure.

It can be that secure lifeboat, there to support you when you need to stay afloat.

Networking is a versatile vehicle. And pretty much however you need to use it, you can. The important thing is that you use it to get you where you're going.

-22-
Potential Friends, Not Prospects

In his book *Who Do You Need To Meet?* professional speaker Rob Thomas encourages you to let go of the notion of selling as you meet others.

Rather, he encourages you to embrace the idea that when you're meeting new people you do so with the intention of discovering a new friend. He goes on to explain that "If you relax your agenda and approach every person as a friend you haven't yet met, the conversation will become more relaxed. From there, you will learn more and create a deeper bond more quickly."

No doubt, if you're in business you need sales today. But that doesn't mean those sales need to come from the next person you meet. Following Thomas' advice of approaching new contacts as friends positions you to build relationships today.

And from those relationships comes the sales that you'll surely need tomorrow.

-23-
The Mousetrap Fable

There is a cute fable about a mouse who is alarmed to learn that the farmer's wife bought a mousetrap. The mouse frantically moves about the farmyard seeking help from his animal neighbors. But none can be bothered.

The chicken says, "This is of no consequence to me." The pig responds, "I can do nothing but pray." And the cow indicates, "I'm sorry but it's no skin off my nose."

But the situation turns when the farmer's wife is bitten by a snake that the trap accidentally snared. As she grows ill and then ultimately dies, the farmer must butcher the chicken, pig, and cow to care for his wife and the many who come to mourn her situation.

The lesson is that no person is completely isolated. Thus, the problems of others will ultimately be your problems, too. So, the next time you learn that someone is troubled, consider lending a hand.

-24-
Gleicher's Formula

You want more out of life, right? Everyone does. Here is the reality: Simply hoping that your situation will change will accomplish nothing. To inspire change, there needs to be more.

In the 1960s, management consultant David Gleicher theorized that change generally doesn't take place unless and until three factors combine to overwhelm the resistance you have to change. Those factors are:

1 - You need to have a significant level of dissatisfaction with your current situation.

2 - You need to have a clear vision for what you want, and that vision must be significantly better than the status quo; and,

3 - For change to occur, you must be clear on what that first definitive step to change is and you must be willing to take it.

Seize more from life. Start by detailing the dissatisfaction you have with your status quo. Then paint a clear picture in your mind as to how great your tomorrow will be. Then, finally, take one step to make it happen.

-25-
R-E-S-P-E-C-T

In his book *MORE: Word of Mouth Referrals, Lifelong Customers and Raving Fans*, renowned professional speaker Matt Ward shares, "Remember, people won't remember what you said, but they will remember how you made them feel."

With that little bit of set up, Ward goes on to share: "Take some time to identify your contact's strengths, and the traits, habits, and characteristics you truly respect them for. Then select the best way to communicate this respect to them."

He encourages you to reach out to these people and share your feelings. In person. Over the phone. In a card. Via e-mail. Make your thoughts clear, genuine, and personal.

Ward also shares examples of things to look for in your contacts that you might respect, including:

- Hustle and Drive
- Commitment
- Positive Attitude
- Financial Acumen
- Daily Habits
- Morning Routine
- Sense of Calm
- Time Management
- Leadership
- Thoughtfulness

Look for one or all of these. But whatever you find, be sure to act.

-26-
Three Pieces of Advice

Theoretical physicist, best-selling author, and renowned cosmologist Stephen Hawking had much to say in his accomplished scientific lifetime. There were, however, three pieces of advice that were anything but technical and anyone can understand them. Those three are:

"One, remember to look up at the stars and not down at your feet. Two, never give up work. Work gives you meaning, and purpose and life is empty without it. Three, if you are lucky enough to find love, remember it is there and don't throw it away."

Whoever you are, whatever you do, you can take advantage of Hawking's three pieces of advice. You can look out, day or night, and be amazed by the world around you. The stars, which includes the sun. Trees. Birds. The wind. You can offer value to the world, even if it's just your corner of the world. And lastly, you can find others to care about, because in time those people will love you too.

-27-
It Works!

Yes, networking – the art and science of building relationships – has been and continues to be the target of much skepticism, as some question the benefits of this soft skill. But know this, networking works.

It may not work exactly how you want it to work. You might be working to get clients, but stumble on that once-in-a-lifetime, perfect vacation. Networking works.

It may not work precisely when you want it to work. You devote weeks to connecting and feel disappointed with the results. Then out of the blue, five years later, something you did in that stint rises up to benefit you. Networking works.

It may not work quite where you want it to work. You spend hours at a tradeshow hoping to make a great connection but come up empty. Then while at the store picking up a few things for home, you happen across that key contact waiting in line with you. It works.

Remember, networking works! Never question that.

-28-
Empathy Versus Compassion

In her book *The Empathy Edge: Harnessing the Value of Compassion as an Engine for Success*, corporate branding expert Maria Ross draws a distinction between empathy and compassion.

Ross shares "The words are often used interchangeably, and they reference related concepts, but they're not exact synonyms. Empathy is a perception, urge or mindset. It has to do with putting yourself in someone else's place and imagining what life is like for them.

"Compassion is activity, decision making, or response. It has to do with taking action that results in kindness towards another."

Ross goes on to elaborate that empathy is essentially an engine. It gives you an idea of what someone is experiencing, seeking, or sensing. Compassion is, however, generally one step further. It's the result.

To summarize, empathy is the feeling. Compassion is putting the love into the situation.

-29-
Find The Right Place

A father handed his son a 200-year-old watch and said "Go to the jewelry store downtown. Tell them that I want to sell it and see what they offer you." The son did, and came home saying, "They offered $150 because it's so old."

The father then said, "Now, go to the pawn shop." Again, the son did. The pawn shop, however, only offered $10 because it looked so worn."

Finally, the father directed his son to go to the museum and show them the watch. The son did and came backed astonished that the curator offered $500,000 for this very rare piece to be included in their precious antiques collection.

The father used this as a teachable moment, saying "Not everyone will appreciate your true value. Don't stay in a place where nobody sees your value. But if you do, don't get angry if you are not appreciated. The right place values you in the right way. Find that place."

-30-
Draw Your Own Conclusions

Everyone has opinions. It is part of being human. And if you live in the free world, you have every right to share those feelings. All in all, opinions are great and generally offer tremendous value. They help you sift through literally volumes of information and dozens of options. They help determine what car to buy or where to find the best cup of coffee.

And while opinions generally provide value, don't rely on them to make a judgment about someone you haven't yet gotten to know. Remember, unlike cars or coffee, there is no means of standard production for the human race. We are all different.

Just because someone has had an unfriendly experience with another and has an unfavorable opinion, does not ensure that your experience will be the same. Remember, you are different. Your perceptions are different. Your tolerances are different. The situation will likely be different. So, draw your own conclusions when it comes to forming an opinion of others.

-31-
Who Is Your Us?

In his book, *No One Gets There Alone*, sports psychologist and mental edge guru Dr. Rob Bell, asks "Who is your us?"

Bell goes on to explain that "Your us is your environment. It's your sphere of influence and the people involved in your interactions and relationships."

He then queries, "Is your us small or large? Is it your school, team, or business? Could it branch out into your community, industry, or conference? Does us include your country, or region, or perhaps the entire world of humankind?"

In short, your us is whomever you come in contact with and influence through your actions and practices. Thus, to become more successful, you need to broaden your us. You need to become other-people focused and be an engine of community and cultural improvement, or even excellence.

As Bell implies, if you focus on your us, you cannot help but become selfless.

-32-
Shine Out of Your Face

This is a reality. It's easy to get down. Life is hard. Relationships can be exhausting. Business can be challenging. No matter who you are, there is always at least one thing not working in your favor.

Despite that, you should remain optimistic and keep wonderful thoughts percolating in your mind. While life is never perfect, if you look at your situation you will find that there is lots to be thankful for. Remember that.

As Roald Dahl, famed author of the story *Charlie and the Chocolate Factory,* once remarked, "If you have good thoughts, they will shine out of your face like sun beams and you will always look lovely."

Life is hard. But as Dahl reminds, you don't have to carry that weight in your mind. And if you shed that mental burden and think positive thoughts, it will change your appearance. And that will serve to draw better things to you. And just like that, life won't be so hard.

-33-
Gracefully Exit

Connecting with people at networking events is great. Whatever the case, do NOT churn the entire event away in a single conversation. And don't have dozens of quick conversations either. That's counterproductive too.

Rather, a great benchmark is to engage in two or three conversations for every hour. That's plenty. Remember, it's not speed dating. Rather, it's building relationships.

Now, so you don't get caught up in a conversation too long, you might consider using one of these statements to help you transition out of a conversation.

1 - "Thanks for your time. I told myself I would meet three interesting people today. I have two more to go."

2 - "There is someone over there that I need to connect with."

3 - "Is there anyone here in particular you would like to meet? I would be glad to introduce you."

Be honest and truthful in using these and they will help you build relationships as you exit conversations.

-34-
Interdependence

In his book *Endless Referrals: Network Your Everyday Contacts Into Sales*, hall of fame speaker Bob Burg makes the point that "we are not dependent on each other; nor are we independent of each other; we are all interdependent with each other."

Burg goes on to elaborate that the true strength you hold really comes through when you realize that all of the people in your network are also part of other people's networks. And these are people that you don't personally know. And that, indirectly, makes each of those people part of your network too.

And you can take that notion out another step. The people who are connected to the people connected to the people you are connected to are, in fact, part of your network. If you take that logic out far enough (which is not too much further), you quickly realize that the entire world is part of your network. And to Burg's point, you are interdependent with it.

-35-
Take Some Blame

In your life, no doubt, from time to time something doesn't work out. The fact of the matter is that under any circumstances, there is probably a little blame in there for you too – even when the culpable person is obvious.

As an example, consider when a child spills milk. While the parent may not be the one who spilled the milk, they can find fault in their own actions or inactions. They could have given them a different cup. They could have not filled their cup so full. They could have done a better job watching over their child.

Think about this next time something goes awry in your world. Even if there is obviously someone else at fault, you can take a little blame yourself (even if only quietly to yourself).

In the long run, people will respect you that much more, which serves to build your relationship with those around you.

-36-
Who Do They Know?

Your house is an asset. So is your ability to work and the experience you have. It all brings you value.

Do you know what else is an asset? Your network. It's true. The people you interact with create value for you. Important contacts. Priceless information. And unique opportunities.

Now, you have a sense as to the value of your house. And you know what your time and expertise is worth too. Right? What's the value of your network?

One way to assess the value of your network is by assessing who do the people you know, know? There are people in your network who hope you'll connect them to the rest of the world. That's nice. And it's great to help them. But the ones who add the most value to you are those who are well-connected and can help you expand your base of contacts. In short, you are best served by building well-connected people into your network.

-37-
Become Worthy of Criticism

Best-selling author and personal development specialist Lewis Howes shared on social media, "You will never be criticized by someone who is doing more than you. You will only be criticized by someone doing less." And then for added emphasis, he asked his audience to read it again.

It's true. People who are really busy and working hard to accomplish things simply don't have time to opine on the efforts or achievements of others. It's only those people with idle time on their hands and unfulfilled dreams that take pause to become critical of others. Don't be like that.

In fact, in a roundabout way what Howes is advocating is that you become worthy of criticism. That is, he is asking you to work hard and accomplish much. So much so, that more and more people can become critical of you. You don't have to listen to them. Just consider them as an indication that you are making your mark on the world.

-38-
The Networking Volunteer

The best way to garner great things from the people around you – contacts, information, and opportunities – is to focus on giving those things first. However, be forewarned: There is not necessarily an immediate payback to the contribution you make to others. It simply takes time for your acts of kindness and sharing your expertise to work its way back to you.

There is, however, a means of getting a more immediate payback from your generous heart. How? Simple. Volunteer.

When you share your time, talent and experience with a charitable organization, social initiative, or community activity you serve yourself in two ways. First, in volunteering you thrust yourself amongst a litany of other new contacts who've also come out of their corner of the world to serve.

Second, when you volunteer, you send a clear message to those inside and outside the endeavor that you're selfless.

So, understanding these benefits, the question you need to address is "Where will you volunteer your time?"

-39-
Be a Wise Person

This wisest people are not the ones with all the answers. The wisest people are those who know they don't have all the answers. And the wisest people know when that is. Furthermore, they are secure enough to know they need outside assistance. And finally, they know where to go looking for the answers they need.

This is the reality: The world has simply become uber complex. Life is full of technology, gizmos and gadgets designed to make life simpler. Moreover, society has become information rich. Everyday there are new and highly beneficial insights and innovations.

As a result, you don't have all the answers. You don't know everything. You aren't supposed to. And so, you don't need to pretend that you do.

But you are connected to all the answers, whatever the question might be. So be one of the wisest people. Tap into the people around you for answers. And if they don't know, surely, they know the person who does.

-40-
Turn Down the Volume

National champion, Heisman Trophy winner and college football TV commentator, Tim Tebow posted on LinkedIn, "We control the volume in whatever voices clamor for our attention. We don't have to give in to or believe everything we hear."

Interesting thought, huh? Around you are many people sharing thoughts and feelings on how you lead your life. "You should do this … if I were you, I'd do that … that won't work, so you better think of something else." It can't hurt to quickly review the substance of each commentary for valuable insight. You just might find some.

But for the bulk of it, keep Tebow's quote in mind. It's okay to turn down the volume on the nay-sayers and those that want to re-frame your life's mission for you. After all, you know your life best. You understand your vision. You know your drive. Only you can feel the burning desire in your heart to create success.

-41-
Invest in Stamps

What are some great investments? Stocks, bonds, and mutual funds? Of course, the equity markets have had a solid track record of consistent gains over time. Real estate? Sure! They aren't making any more land and people will always need a place to live.

Here's one you've probably not thought of, however. Stamps. Yes, United States first class postage. No doubt, stamps might not sound like a sexy investment. And you might not be able to envision a great rate of return. But it's true. The return is awesome.

No, this is not to advocate starting a stamp collection. Rather, it's to encourage you to get in the habit of purchasing first class postage and using it to send out notes and cards to those in your network.

You see, these small personal gestures will serve to land you opportunities, retain great clients and keep you on the radar of strategic partners. And these returns all come from investments in stamps.

-42-
Real World Success Online

To be successful at networking via social media, you need to follow the same practices as you would networking in the real world.

In the real world, every contact has opportunity. This is the same with online. You should never 'dis' someone because of their stature in life. You just never know with whom they are connected.

In the real world, a great way to achieve networking success is by giving to others. The same holds true for social media. Find ways to add value to your contacts.

In the real world, a flurry of networking once or twice a year generally yields very little. This sort of binge networking does no better when it comes to social media. Rather, commit to taking moderate, but consistent action.

In the real world, building strong relationships takes time. With online social networking, the same is true. Be patient.

Remember these practices when networking online and you'll achieve real world success.

-43-
A Daily Mantra Routine

Kimberly Rice, a marketing consultant and author of *Rainmaker Roadmap: A Step-by-Step Guide to Building a Prosperous Business*, remains grounded and positive in life, while still driving forward. How? She shares that she uses a daily mantra routine with three components.

First, she reminds herself that "Life is happening *for* me, not *to* me."

Then, she devotes 16 seconds each and every day to saying, "I am positively expecting, ready to receive and manifest great abundance in all areas of my life."

And then finally, Rice completes the following sentence, "I am so happy and grateful now that …!

What's your daily mantra routine? How do you remain grounded in the chaos that life can bring? What serves to keep you positive? Where do you find the inspiration to keep driving forward?

Don't have one? Consider borrowing Rice's. No doubt, she'll be so happy and grateful that you did.

-44-
Give By Getting

They say, "It is better to give than to receive." This statement is true. But it's not because giving is the right thing to do. No. This statement is true because there is truly more joy in giving to someone else than receiving from them.

Knowing this, you should set about giving more. Give more referrals. Make more introductions. Share more information and opportunities. From time to time, however, someone might beat you to the punch, giving something to you first. This serves to flip the "give first; get second" mantra on its ear, right?

What should you do? Answer: Nothing. You see, by accepting their generosity, you are in a sense giving back to them, as you're allowing them the joy of giving.

As such, the gift of receiving from others in a genuine and appreciative manner is a very real part of altruism. So as much as you should make giving to others a habit, you also get good at getting too.

-45-
10 Steps to Working The Event

Here are 10 easy steps to successfully work the networking event.

One, avoid the biggest failure. Show up.

Two, come with an attitude of wanting to help others.

Three, don't worry about who you connect with, as every contact has opportunity.

Four, position yourself in the room where the people are.

Five, initiate contact by making meaningful eye contact, smiling, and saying hello.

Six, when someone stops to talk, shake their hand, offer your name, and clarify their name after they say it.

Seven, engage in conversation. Start with small talk. And never pitch or ask self-serving questions.

Eight, as they talk, listen. Ask clarifying questions. Share relevant comments. Look for things you have in common.

Nine, after a bit, move the conversation back to small talk and suggest you two continue the conversation in a different setting.

And ten - follow up. E-mail to set up coffee or lunch. And send a handwritten note.

-46-
Ride The Waves

Author, professor and renowned social science researcher Dr. Adam Grant shared on Twitter, "We can't always control the waves of emotion that crash into us. But we can learn to ride them more gracefully. Emotional intelligence starts with choosing not to be victims of our moods. By noticing what causes them, we find clues on how to change them—or at least manage them."

As Grant implies, life is hard. Yes, you can look backwards and have a sense as to all the answers and what you should have done. It's all so obvious. Going forward, however, things seem to come a million miles per hour. A good day can turn into a bad one in an instant.

While you can't control the waves that come at you, you can choose how you'll ride them. No matter what, you can decide to ride life's waves with an optimistic and determined demeanor.

-47-
Dedicated To a Better World

Hall of fame football coach and namesake of the Super Bowl Champion trophy, Vince Lombardi once said: "After all the cheers have died down and the stadium is empty … the enduring thing that is left is the dedication to doing with our lives the very best we can to make the world a better place in which to live."

You know what? We all have a career path. Entrepreneurs. Sales Representations. Professionals. Executives. Teachers. Administrators. Everyone has a role in adding value to society, even though chances are you're not a professional football player.

But as Lombardi implies, beyond your chosen vocation, you also have an obligation to somehow make the world a better place. Perhaps it's through volunteering at a charitable organization or social initiative. Perhaps it something less formal, like keeping an eye out for an elderly neighbor or quietly mentoring a recent graduate.

Whatever it is, you need to be dedicated to a better world.

-48-
Don't Talk to Strangers

Walk into any event and you know what you'll find? Strangers. People you've never seen before. And even if you have, you may not know their names. You probably don't know their stories. In short, you really know nothing about them.

At this point remember the advice given to you by parents, teachers, and den mothers: "Don't talk to strangers!" Seriously, don't talk to strangers. Rather, without haste, walk up to such a person, offer your hand to shake, clearly state your name, and then ask for theirs.

In so doing, the person is no longer a stranger and, therefore, is fair game for conversation. Heck, you could even meet them for a cup of coffee.

If you think about it, quickly converting these strangers into friendly new connections is an important part of your continued success and personal development. After all, you can't build your professional life or expand your social horizons solely on the backs of those you already know.

-49-
Rekindle Your Sense of Humor

In his newsletter, *Positive Psychology Tools with the Biggest Bang for Your Buck,* relationship expert and executive coach Dr. John Schinnerer shares that a great way to stay happy and healthy is to cultivate a sense of humor. Schinnerer adds that this simple (and fun) trait increases your chances of living past the age of 70.

But beyond better overall life, he reminds us that people like to be around others who are quick to laughter. So, having a sense of humor is great for building personal and professional relationships. This in time, serves your bottom line.

Finally, your sense of humor is based in how you think and is something you can learn to develop. Schinnerer suggests that you practice amusing yourself by training yourself to look at routine situations in new, creative ways.

Yes, laughing is great for a long happy and healthy life … and business.

-50-
Get Your Brand Back

No doubt, you've envisioned the personal brand you want for yourself. It likely involves reliability, generosity and being considered hard working. Life, however, doesn't always unfold the way you'd like.

Maybe you find that you won't be able to meet a deadline. Or resources are short, and you can't contribute what you want. Or perhaps you simply don't have the energy to put in the effort you normally do. But it's okay.

Remember that championship teams lose games from time to time. The world's smartest people don't get all the right answers (and can sometimes do some awfully dumb things). Even the most beloved companies have a bad year (or years).

These setbacks do not change who they are and what they strive for. Likewise, neither should your setbacks. Remember, it is never too late to get your actions back in lockstep with the vision you have for your personal brand.

-51-
Little Windows of Pain

When you think of success, you seldom equate it with pain. But nevertheless, success in any area involves a certain degree of pain.

Working toward getting into and surviving college life reveals the pain of hard work and discipline. The same is true of any other venture, whether it's starting and growing a business or profession or achieving and maintaining a healthy mind and body. Each of these involves the pain of hard work and discipline.

But what if you choose not to endure the pain associated with success? There is still pain. You see, if you fail to endure the pain associated with hard work and discipline, then you experience the pain associated with regret. The pain of regret, however, is forever, as you can never shed the pain of unrealized potential.

In contrast, the pain of hard work and disciple associated with success is temporary. This hardship only appears in tiny, little windows of time. Because once you achieve success, the pain dissipates and is replaced with an overwhelming sense of satisfaction.

-52-
Quell Your Emotions

In her book *The Resilient Leader: Life-Changing Strategies to Overcome Today's Turmoil and Tomorrow Uncertainty*, business growth architect Christine Perakis shares her strategy for overcoming debilitating fear as a Category 5 hurricane raged around her.

She said, "Alone and off the grid, the only tools I had were a pen and paper. A tiny voice in my head said, 'Use this experience, learn from it, start writing while you can still remember everything that is happening.'"

Perakis shares that writing kept her mind focused and forced her to engage the problem-solving section of her brain. And that served to naturally calm and quiet her emotions. Despair simply could not set in.

She goes on to remind you that storms occur in your life too – if not now, then for sure one day. She encourages you to develop the habit of writing in those moments, even if just making a list, as that will help you better solve what is coming at you.

-53-
One Brain

Take a moment. With your hands, reach up and grab your head. Inside your hard-shelled noggin is your brain.

The human brain, weighing in at only a few pounds, is the most amazing thing ever known. Beyond being responsible for the functioning of your entire body, it is a processing center for all your thoughts and feelings. And from those come your judgments and actions.

Know this, however, while you might have both a personal and professional life, you only have one brain. It processes everything the same. It builds trust the same. It grapples with betrayal and despair the same.

So, if you are ever at a loss as to how you deal with a challenging professional relationship, remember you only have one brain. Reflect upon on when you've dealt with something similar in your personal life. Chances are, therein will lie the answer. Somewhere in that one brain.

-54-
Response Time Matters

When someone reaches out to you for whatever reason - a referral, an answer, an introduction, whatever – what they need is important. They might not need you to respond within the hour, but they certainly appreciate not being put off for days or even weeks.

Thus, you should promptly return phone calls and respond to emails. Sure, this is good business etiquette. But equally important, this is an effective means of building relationships.

You see, when you make a reasonable priority of the important things in other people's lives, you send a clear message. One that says, "You matter ... I'm here for you ... I've got your back." And people can't help but know, like and trust those who communicate that message.

So, in a quiet moment, ask yourself what is your policy for responding to calls and emails in a timely manner? Then ponder how you could up the ante on your policy and better build your network in the process.

-55-
Become a Pitchman

From a young age, no doubt the notion of sharing was drilled into your head. Share candy. Share a seat on the bus. Share time with people that matter. But now social media gives you a whole new avenue for sharing.

As word-of-mouth referral consultant Matt Ward advises in his book *MORE … Word of Mouth Referrals, Lifelong Customers and Raving Fans*: "Share newsworthy updates about your contact's business on your social media accounts and tag them. By tagging your contact, you let them know that you have shared their news. Sharing their content demonstrates that you care about your contact and their business." After all, if they posted it, they want to get the word out.

And as Ward implies, this is a very small effort that has a massive impact in the heart and mind of your contact. It's something that takes mere moments to do but will be online forever. So, become a pitchman for your contacts online.

-56-
Tiny Habits

John Dryden, England's first Poet Laureate and 17th century literary critic, is credited with saying, "We first make our habits and then our habits make us." And there is much truth in this, just as there is much truth in 1,000 other similar quotes made since.

Great quotes on habits, however, do not make habits. You have to intentionally work on them. One way to do that is to follow the teachings of Stanford University behavioral scientist BJ Fogg.

Fogg shared that one incredibly easy way to create a habit is to take a small (almost laughable) baby step towards the larger habit you'd like to instill. For example, to embrace the habit of regularly flossing your teeth, you'd start by simply flossing a single tooth each day. And from there, the larger habit will build.

So, what's that one great habit you want to master? Identify one tiny step that you could master en route to it. Then simply start there.

-57-
Beyond The Transactional

Somehow, when people talk about the benefits of networking, it conjures up this image: Someone comes to you who needs the service you provide or the product you sell. You come through for them at a five-star level, culminating with the transaction being settled financially.

And yes, this is definitely a benefit of networking. However, it is only one of many. For example, someone could tip you off to a great, inexpensive destination vacation where you can relax and recharge, then resume bringing your "A" game to your work. That's a benefit of networking.

Or a contact might share some information that serves to help you navigate a challenging professional dilemma. You can credit that to networking too.

Your network can also provide you with encouragement, emotional support, and additional contacts. Suffice it to say, there is a lot that networking can do beyond leading you to transactional encounters with customers and clients.

-58-
Out of the Trash

On her *Networking Ninja Series*, Alison Henderson, body language expert and owner of Moving Image Consulting asks, "Are you throwing your introduction in the trash?" She explains that if you introduce yourself at a networking event or meeting in a ho-hum fashion, you are essentially discarding an opportunity.

She goes on to advise that whenever you have a chance to share who you are and what you do, your job is to interest someone enough to want more. Create intrigue so they follow up with a question. Or imply such value that they seek you out to get together another time.

In other words, give your audience (whether it's one or 1,000) a reason to step forward or lean forward in their chair and say, "I need to talk to this person." This will keep you top of mind and your potential new connection out of the trash.

-59-
The Sweetest Sound

Your name is important to you. Right? You want others not only to remember it, but to pronounce it correctly too. That's a reasonable expectation for the people who want a place in your life.

And so, think about it. If your name is important to you, then it's not such a stretch that someone else's name is just as important to them.

Knowing this, one of the best ways to build a relationship with a new connection is to make their name a priority. This indicates to them that you value the connection with them and that they have made a significant impression on you. In short, this simple act makes them feel important, which serves to endear them to you, thus building the relationship.

As Dale Carnegie remarked in his book *How to Win Friends and Influence People*, "Remember that a person's name is to him or her the sweetest and most important sound in any language."

-60-
Relationship Momentum

Think of building a great relationship like pushing a car: You have to work really hard to get it rolling. Once you get it going, however, you only have to exert mild force to keep it moving. With relationships the mild force to keep it all moving involves three things.

One. Give. Take the time to understand where they want to go, then help them get there, even if just in a small way.

Two. Ask. Ask for referrals and introductions. Ask for information, opportunities, and advice. Your network wants to help you. Let them.

And three. Appreciate. No matter what your network does for you, thank them. If a referral goes nowhere, thank them anyway. Remember, appreciation is a wonderful motivator. Dole it out and people will do whatever it takes to get more.

Just like pushing that car, don't let your efforts wane as it's important to maintain that relationship momentum.

-61-
Different Rivers; Different People

Experience is a wonderful thing. It can give you a leg up on what you're facing today. It'll give you a sense as to how you might tackle a challenge or capitalize on an opportunity.

While experience will help you, know that you can never completely rely on it. Yesterday was a day ago. And while today's situation might be somewhat similar it's not completely the same. And for that matter, neither are you.

So, you need to approach life day by day, eager to learn something new. And you need to be ever ready to pivot to a new way of thinking or approaching things.

As you venture into similar settings or face up to comparable situations remember the words of Heraclitus – a fifth century BC Greek philosopher: "No person ever steps in the same river twice, for it's not the same river and they're not the same person."

-62-
Embrace Mistakes

Considered one of the most influential and important authors of the 20th century, James Joyce once remarked that "Mistakes are the portals of discovery."

This Irish novelist, short story writer, and literary critic knew that there is little learning associated with playing it safe and never being wrong. Your best achievements and your biggest breakthroughs are somewhere on the other side of disappointing mistakes.

Through potentially embarrassing blunders you learn about your own resolve. You find impactful insights. And you uncover the people in your life you can truly count on.

Embrace your mistakes. They're an indication that you're on your way to something wonderful. They're a hint as to where and how you can accomplish great things.

So, instead of looking at mistakes as your enemy, see them as that wonderful friend; the one who provides some tough love as they guide you to the path of greater success.

-63-
Walking On the Moon

Apollo astronaut Gene Cernan, the last man to step on the moon, had a modest upbringing in the Chicago suburbs and spent most of his summers on his grandparent's farm with no electricity. With that background he often posed this somewhat rhetorical question to encourage his grandchildren: "I walked on the moon. What can't you do?"

If you think about it, that's an inspiring question. No one on the planet is born into such a position of prominence that they are entitled to achieve great things. Rather, greatness is earned.

It's earned by having the courage to dream and have a vision for yourself. It's earned through hard work and continually challenging yourself to achieve more. And it's earned by persisting and driving through those times when success doesn't seem possible.

Now think about your life. Chances are you had humble beginnings too. So, walking on the moon is certainly possible, isn't it?

-64-
Tribe Quality

In her book *Becoming Competition Proof: Stand Out and Overcome Competition Through Generosity, Service and Added Value,* adventure coach Berta Medina Garcia challenges you to ask yourself these questions:

"What are you contributing to your tribe? What is your tribe contributing to you? How are you helping each other grow and achieve? Who is keeping you accountable and holding you to a higher standard? Who wants more for you? Who is calling you out when you need to be called out and empowering and encouraging you for more?"

She goes on to imply that if you don't like the answers you get, then your tribe is likely not serving you. But this may also mean that you aren't serving them either. It might be time to find or build a new tribe. Or at a minimum swap some people for others.

These are not easy decisions. And you should think through things carefully. Remember, the quality of your tribe reflects the quality of your contribution to it.

-65-
No Short Cuts

Here is a simple formula for landing great clients. Go to an event. A business afterhours. A Chamber function. Or perhaps a tradeshow. That's it.

Well, not quite. At the event, strike up a conversation with someone. That's it. Of course, it's got to be sufficient that the two of you want to continue it another time over coffee or lunch. But that's it.

But certainly, you have to go to that follow-up appointment and continue the process of learning about them as well as sharing about yourself. And there you go.

Except that, through that conversation, you'll have built a relationship with your new acquaintance. And from there, they will introduce you to other wonderful people.

Keep in mind, these new connections aren't the great clients. But they will lead to other connections. And in time, that will lead to great clients.

Now, the good news is that this is a simple formula to getting great clients. The bad news is that there are no short cuts.

-66-
Take Control

Being a successful entrepreneur or professional is not an easy proposition. Having a successful career isn't any easier, truth be told.

Part of what makes it difficult is that so much is out of your control. You can't really control who will hire you or take on your services. You can't control what people will say about you. And you can't control who is going to invite you into their world.

The only thing that you really have control over is you. You can control how you face up to adversity. You can control how hard you work. You can control how much energy you devote to your craft. You can control the competitive advantages that you bring to market. You can control how you show up and what you add to the world.

So, get after it. Take control of what you can. That initiative will lead to great things.

-67-
Nourishing Your Network

In his book *Be Connected*, relationship builder, dynamic speaker and social media professional Terry Bean asks: "Are you nourishing your network so it can nourish you?"

He goes on to share that if you're disappointed with your networking results, you first need to examine what you've done to deserve anything positive from the people around. To make this assessment, Bean offers some questions to ponder:

Are you providing opportunity to your network?

Does your network understand the value you have to offer? Do you understand theirs?

Have you helped your network identify your ideal client as well as strategic partners? Do you know theirs?

Ponder these questions. And if the answers are less than ideal, don't be surprised if your results are less than ideal, too. How you interact with your network has a direct impact on what you get from it.

As Bean reminds, networking takes work. It's even right there in the word.

-68-
I Know the Face, But...

Be honest. You've forgotten someone's name before. Everyone has. In fact, some more often than others.

Certainly, the best means of dealing with this is working hard to remember name in the first place. That, however, is easier said than done.

So, next time you forget a name, do not complicate the situation by faking your way through a conversation. And certainly, don't just avoid the conversation all together.

In this moment, the best thing to do is simply admit to your minor shortcoming with something like: "I'm sorry. I heard your name, but it seems to have slipped out of my head." Or "I am sorry. I remember you, but at this moment I can't recall your name."

You will find that people are very forgiving. Remember, everyone has done this. Plus, as a result of your honesty, they might like you more. For sure, however, life will become a whole lot less stressful.

-69-
Rise After the Fall

Ralph Waldo Emerson, essayist, lecturer, philosopher, and champion of individualism during the middle part of the 19th century once said, "Our greatest glory is not in never failing, but in rising up every time we fail."

While Emerson uttered those words around the time of the Civil War, that line has never gone out of style. And it's never been truer.

Life is hard. Business is hard. There is no easy path to success. If you're at it long enough, you're going to fail. You're going to fail to meet quota. You're going to fail to get the promotion. You're going to fail to meet a thousand different goals and objectives.

So what? Get up! Dust yourself off. And continue on. Those are the glorious moments of life. You know. That moment where you've been figuratively gut punched and are on your knees, but you have not been stopped. You're temporarily down, but you rise up and carry on.

-70-
Trust Perfect Timing

On the *Networking Rx* podcast, JV Crum, III, mentor to aspiring high-level earners and host of the top ranked *Conscious Millionaire Show*, shared a personal mantra that has helped to drive his decades of success: Trust Perfect Timing.

To explain, let's say you really want to meet that local business icon at a particular event. However, through a variety of circumstances it doesn't happen. That's okay. The timing wasn't right. But when the connection is finally made the situation will be optimal.

Or you hope to land that A-list client to round out your quarterly goals. But it doesn't happen. That's okay. It wasn't supposed to happen. For whatever reason the timing wasn't right. Perhaps you aren't ready and having that client at this time would have led to a debacle. And if it is to be, when it happens, you'll be best situated to serve.

Essentially, Crum encourages you to have faith that things happen when they're supposed to.

-71-
Keeping Score

This is a reality of life: We keep score. In sports there are points and goals. In business, sales and profits. And in personal lives there are academic credentials and net worth. We keep score, as it's almost natural to tally up progress.

Despite this, don't make this practice part of your daily networking activities. That is, you should not account for how much you've done for others.

First, this goes against the notion of "giving and expecting nothing in return." Plus, it's impractical. Your roster of contacts is vast, and the ongoing exchange of referrals, introductions and information is immense.

And, even if you could quantify the tally of "who has done what," why would you? After all, the exchange in any relationship ebbs and flows. Thus, the score could never be "all tied up."

When you network, you need to simply do for others and trust that whatever you do will find its way back to you – because it almost always does.

-72-
Networking Event On Steroids

No doubt you've been to networking events. A business after-hours. An open house. Or a tradeshow. Do you know what? That's what social media is. It's nothing more than a networking event. One on steroids, however.

First, there are hundreds of millions of people participating and they're scattered all over the world, unlike that local event with a few hundred participants just from your area code.

Second, social media is running 24 hours a day, 7 days a week, 365 days a year. You can't say that about traditional networking events. They're not continuously operating and you can't just drop in as you watch the big game, or when you can't sleep or during a major holiday.

Finally, with social media you can know a ton about people before you start to converse. That's not possible with a local in-person event.

So, approach social media as if it were just another networking event, but remember it's worldwide and immense, continuously operating and rich with searchable information.

-73-
Build a Mental Scrapbook

In a newsletter entitled *Positive Psychology Tools with the Biggest Bang for Your Buck,* executive coach and relationship expert Dr. John Schinnerer shares that a wonderful way of increasing your happiness is reliving memories of enjoyable times in your life.

No doubt you have a treasure trove of happy memories from your life. Ponder for a moment. There were fun times with great friends. There was that wonderful family vacation. There was a wedding, perhaps yours. The birth of a child. Your favorite team's improbable win. And dozens of other milestones and moments imbedded in your memory.

As Schinnerer indicates, you can increase your happiness by simply reflecting on any of these. But he goes on to make the point that going forward, you should make a mental note when something wonderful happens. Building this mental scrapbook allows you to more easily revisit and dwell upon those things that drive your happiness.

-74-
Make Them Feel Important

To most effectively build relationships, your goal should not be to get people to think more highly of you. It should be to get them to think more highly of themselves.

Think about that. People want to associate with those who bring them value. But value doesn't just come from referrals and introductions that get them clients or career opportunities. While no one will argue that those things are not important, equally important are things that serve to build someone else's self-esteem.

Most everyone, from your struggling college student to an established local business icon, has insecurities about who there really are and what they contribute to the world. So never underestimate how your compliments and words of reassurance will have a positive impact on them.

As Mary Kay Ash, founder of Mary Kay Cosmetics put it, "Everyone has an invisible sign hanging from their neck saying, 'Make Me Feel Important!' Never forget this message when working with people."

-75-
Types of Social Media Posts

Social media platforms give you the opportunity to make posts. That said, not all posts are the same. They come in one of three categories.

First is the update. Imagine having a publicist. Someone who tracks your every move and reports it to the world like you were some Hollywood star. Well, via social media you can share on your profile the things you are doing, enlightening others.

Second is adding value. Remember people want to associate with those that have something to offer. Through your social media posts, you can provide value to your network by offering information or sharing insights.

Finally, there are posts that evoke discussion or encourage conversation. These types of posts create interaction and interaction generally leads to value. So, think about engaging your online network by asking a question, soliciting feedback, or creating a forum for discussion.

Whether you share an update, add value, or create discussion, make the most of your social media posts.

-76-
Mind Over Moments

In an article in the July-August 2020 edition of *Success Magazine*, entrepreneur and speaker Anne Grady shares about her book *Mind Over Moment: Harness the Power of Resilience*.

She explains that 'mind over moment' is a science-based strategy she developed. It utilizes mindfulness to help you become aware of your thoughts, feelings, and habits. The purpose is to help you steer yourself toward better responses and outcomes amidst crisis or challenge.

Some ideas that Grady shares are:

Tame negative self-talk by acknowledging what the voices in your head are spewing and reminding yourself that it's not true.

Or, within your current predicament, find something to laugh about. Something ironic. Something whimsical. Anything to lighten the mood.

Or find something to be grateful for. No matter the situation, there is always something to be thankful about. Focus on that and what it can do for you.

As Grady implies no matter what, your mind can take control of any moment.

-77-
What's Your Name?

Whether you consider yourself a master at remembering names or currently aspiring to that status, the reality is that at one time or another, your memory will fail you. It is at this frustrating and often embarrassing moment that you will likely recognize the face but, for whatever reason, cannot place the name.

When this happens, you have several options, but there is really only one proper course of action. Simply fess up and ask, "What's your name?"

Listen, avoiding the person does nothing to build the relationship. And faking your way through a conversation doesn't correct the problem either. Plus, it serves to make you look foolish.

In admitting your memory lapse, you can blame it on anything you'd like, such as age, a busy week or temporary confusion. Whatever the case, by acknowledging your forgetfulness, you'll get a reminder.

In so doing, and this is key, you indicate to the person that their name is important. And with that, even though you've forgotten their name, you've served to build the relationship.

-78-
Enjoy The Little Things

Famed American writer Kurt Vonnegut once remarked, "Enjoy the little things in life, for one day you'll look back and realize they were the big things."

Yes, life is such that attention is drawn to the big things. Milestone birthdays. Graduations. Weddings. Children. Promotions. And ultimately retirement. But those are often fleeting moments, providing merely flashes of happiness.

Lasting happiness, however, comes from the little things. The ones you might tend to overlook. Family movie night. Enjoying meals together. Playing games with friends. A good cup of coffee and that morning paper. Sitting around a campfire. Watching fireworks. Star gazing on a clear summer night. A long walk amongst nature. Listening to that music that makes you smile. A big warm hug on a chilly winter day.

You might tend to overlook these moments as sources of joy in your life. But these are the things that make life worth living. Best of all, opportunities for these moments are all around you.

-79-
Bringing Immense Value

Bob Burg, hall of fame speaker, author, and champion of creating influential relationships, shared on Twitter, "In a 'truly' free market, there's only one way to profit: by providing immense value to those who 'willingly choose' to buy from you. How are you providing - and communicating - such an immensely value?"

This is such a great encapsulation of how business works. But it is also a great summary for, really, how life happens. Getting wonderful people in your world, which is the equivalent of landing awesome clients, starts with you being a great person. And becoming that great person involves bringing immense value to your world.

So, how can you bring immense value to your world? Sure, business-related things, such as referrals, introductions, and opportunities, are something. But more important are the human things, such as caring, being empathetic and being there in the moments when people need you most.

-80-
A Fulfilled Life

There is no such thing as a fully grown tree. Why? Because any tree's ongoing mission each and every day is to reach and expand to gather in more sun light. As such, a tree grows until the day it dies.

To reach your potential, you need to be like a tree. Each and every day look for opportunities to develop your skills. Become more proficient at writing, using technology and communicating.

Each and every day grow your mind. This is not done simply by becoming more knowledgeable but by developing the wisdom of how you use that knowledge. Do this by reading appropriate material, listening to podcasts and attending professional programs.

Each and every day, grow your network by building relationships with the people you already know, and endeavoring to meet new people as well.

Commit to lifelong growth in these areas of personal development. In the end, you will not just have a full life, but a fulfilled life, too.

-81-
Cooking Your Own Stone Soup

Networking is about giving. It is not about waiting for someone to do something for you and then finding a way to return the favor.

Just like the traveling peddler in the *Story of Stone Soup* who sparked passion for giving by simply contributing an innocuous stone to a cauldron of boiling water, you need to take it upon yourself to create an atmosphere of giving wherever you go.

If you're looking for people to like, comment and share your posts, take the initiative do so first. If you're looking for introductions to wonderful strategic partners, start by introducing others to their sought-after strategic partners. If you're looking for great referrals or opportunities to grow your profession or career, begin by doing those things for others.

With any of these, lean into your effort. Make helping others a priority and don't keep score. In time, you'll have the people around you contributing to your metaphorical Stone Soup creation.

-82-
Fear's Greatest Adversary

In her book *Becoming Competition Proof*, adventure coach Berta Medina makes the point that most fears are predictive. That is, you don't really know if something will bring a painful outcome; you simply foreshadow that it will.

For example, you don't know for sure that reaching out to the local business icon or walking into a networking event will leave you with a feeling of being rejected. However, your mind strongly reminds you that it could be the case. You don't know for sure that asking for a promotion could leave you with no job at all. But, again, your brain focuses on that negative outcome.

It are these predictions that can leave you frozen with trepidation. But, as Medina shares, "If prediction is fear's greatest ally, then action is its greatest adversary."

As she summarizes, "When you take action on your fears you prove to yourself once and for all, whether it was worth being scared or not."

-83-
Raise the Lid

In his book, *The 21 Irrefutable Laws Of Leadership*, leadership expert John C. Maxwell introduces the concept of The Law Of The Lid. Simply put, The Law Of The Lid states that everyone has leadership ability and will only attract as followers those with equal or lesser leadership ability.

Through personal growth, you can improve your leadership ability and effectively elevate your 'lid'. What ensues is that you increase the number of people that will potentially follow your leadership.

What is true of leadership is also true of building a network. The more value you have to offer, the more others are attracted to associate with you.

So, you can expand the sphere of your network by growing the people you interact with, by increasing the information you have access to and by uncovering more opportunities. Each of these serves to raise the lid on your network.

-84-
Life's Not Fair

Look around. There are people with more money. A better house. That car you'd love to be seen in. Some people seem to be able to eat anything (or everything) and never gain a pound. Some have perfect hair. Others, a really attractive smile. A few have both.

Some people seem to have a wonderful, carefree business or career. Some seem to not be able to make a wrong move. Some people just have it made. In summary, some people just seem to be better off.

Remember, though, you were born into a completely different set of circumstances with a singularly unique DNA. As such, life is "not fair." But then, no one ever said it would be.

As much as life is "not fair," it is "not unfair" either. That is, there is no grand conspiracy against you. If you're listening to this, you have the freedom and access to information and opportunities to do something great with your life. So, get after it.

-85-
Play To Win

Corporate psychologist and motivational speaker Tim Shurr shared on his *How To Be Mesmerizing* podcast:

> "Do you know what happens when you play not to lose? You lose! I spent the first half of my life, waiting for the next bad thing to happen. Many times, bad things did happen because whatever you look for hard enough, you will find! These hurtful experiences reinforced my fearful beliefs, and the coping strategies I developed to deal with the anxiety only made things worse. I was in a destructive cycle and had no idea how to get out of it!"

But he goes on to explain that if you play to win, the outcomes are vastly different. When you play to win, great outcomes are almost inevitable.

And Shurr indicates that playing to win is simply a mindset. Setting lofty goals. Having a big vision for yourself. Taking small, calculated risks. And using failures as steppingstones. In short, if you play to win, you will.

-86-
Knight In Shining Armor

Wouldn't this be great? You meet that person who, in your mind, is the epitome of success. After a short conversation, you hit it off and this person takes you under their wing – feeding you all sorts of great business referrals, valuable information, and wonderful business contacts. They'd be like a knight in shining armor coming along to rescue you from the issues and challenges of business.

But here is another thought. Rather than hoping this person comes into your world, why not become that person in someone else's world? Think about it.

You'll become known as "that special person" and then everyone will want to meet you. Plus, as you serve your role helping others, you'll inspire others to want to give back to you.

So, as you continue networking, throw your shoulders back, raise your chin and embark upon it with heroic confidence. You are here to save the day. Find someone and life up their world. Remember, you are the knight in shining armor.

-87-
Nothing Alone

It's a common daydream. You, alone, against incredible odds, land a key client. Or perhaps your idea helps your employer become substantially more profitable. Or perhaps you and your business are profiled in *Inc.*, *Fortune* or *The Wall Street Journal*.

But it is not wishful thinking that these achievements can be made. You are well educated, work hard and are considered an expert. In short, your actions and attitudes make achievements inevitable.

And it is not fiction that these achievements will come despite amazing obstacles. Business is tough. Your clients or customers are continually being pursued by competitors. Great ideas on which to capitalize seem fewer and farther between. No doubt whatever you do will be done against incredible odds.

It is a fantasy, however, to believe that these achievements could ever be attained alone. Rather, each step of the way – whether you know it or are willing to admit it – your network provided assistance. You've done nothing alone. And never forget that.

-88-
Bend The Universe

Terry Bean, social architect and founder of the Detroit area's Motor City Connect, shared in his book *Be Connected: Strategies To Attract The Right Opportunities, Connections and Clients Through Effective Networking*:

"A couple of interesting things happen when you give a referral. The first one is that the recipient is likely to go out of their way to reciprocate. The second thing that happens is that the universe bends to make sure that those who do good have good done unto them."

Bean goes on to explain that when you do something for someone, they are highly attuned to opportunities for you. But you also increase the odds that you will receive something from a totally difference source.

None of this is magic. But when you help someone, it's not done in a vacuum. Others bear witness to or learn of it. And those others want to be part of your world. As Bean implies, you have bent the Universe in your favor.

-89-
Knocking Over a Domino

According to Debra Fine, author of *The Fine Art Of Small Talk*, "A little chit chat with someone is the verbal equivalent of knocking over the first domino. It starts a chain reaction with all kinds of implications for our lives."

Isn't it true? Nothing great ever materialized out of getting right down to "brass tacks." Think about it. That wonderful person in your life did not start with "Will you marry me?" You didn't land that five-star client by saying, "What do I need to do to get your business?"

Life's greatest personal and professional adventures started with nothing more than seemingly unnoteworthy comments like, "You have an interesting accent. Where are you from?" Or, "That's a remarkable tie. Where did you find it?"

With Fine's advice and those thoughts, go talk to someone. Who? Anyone, really. And what should you talk about? Just about anything. Say or ask whatever to knock over that first domino.

-90-
The Dark Side of Motivation

Much of your success in life depends upon your ability to motivate others. You motivate people to associate with you. You motivate them to give you referrals. You motivate them to become your partner. You motivate them to do all sorts of things. Motivation is essential to a healthy social and professional life.

That said, you need to remember that motivation is simply finding objectives that would be good for both you and others. From there, you need to encourage those others to undertake the actions with you, so that together you achieve the objectives.

There is a dark side to motivation, however. This happens when you motivate others toward goals and objectives that only serve your interests and are knowingly not in the best interest of the other person.

This brand of motivation is known as manipulation. And while the temptation to manipulate may present itself, you need to resist it. Just using it once can serve to destroy trust forever.

-91-
Take Time To Thank

As word-of-mouth referral consultant Matt Ward advises in his book *MORE ... Word of Mouth Referrals, Lifelong Customers and Raving Fans*: "You can never thank people enough for their time, attention, or effort whether in person or using other means, like e-mails, texts or even cards. Pausing for moments to express gratitude is well worth the effort."

Ward goes on to recommend you prepare by purchasing a big package of thank you cards and keeping them handy. That way, after meeting with a new contact, client or even a vendor you're ready and able to share words of thanks.

And it's important to note that what you write doesn't have to be long-winded. A short note is plenty. Actually, that's best.

Ward recommends that while there doesn't need to be much to this, you're best to personalize the note to create a positive impression. He further recommends that you avoid generic content, as that detracts from the overall impact.

-92-
Life's Ups and Downs

When things are going well, you tend to overlook a lot. Things like that rude prospective client. Or that surprise invoice with a shocking total. Or missing your connecting flight.

But when things are not going your way, even the smallest irritation feels like a gigantic annoyance. Things like slow Internet. Or the vendor who's one minute late. Or coffee that's just a little bit off.

None of this is shocking, is it? When the flow of life is moving in your direction, you feel confident, in control, and almost unbeatable. But when it's not, you get the sensation that things are slipping away, almost as if life could be falling apart.

Here is the reality: Neither of these perspectives are true. You are never invincible. And you're never on the brink of destruction. Whenever you experience the high or the low, you need to remind yourself of that. In either case, take a deep breath and relax. Eventually, the situation will swing back towards normal.

-93-
Never-Ending Value

If you want to be successful at growing a strong network and building the underlying relationships that hold it all together, you have to add value to the people with whom you associate. The reality is that most people are tripped up in their networking efforts by underperforming at this. And some outright fail.

There is, however, a simple means of adding value to others and it's wrapped up in one simple mantra: "Everyone you know can benefit from someone else you already know."

Think about it. Pluck 20 people at random out of your contact list. Examine the list. How many of those people know each other? It's unlikely that anyone knows everyone else on the list. In fact, a large percentage likely don't know anyone else.

This lack of connectiveness represents amazing potential to add value to others. You simply need to figure out who could benefit by knowing who and then act by making introductions. If you adopt this mantra, you'll have a means for creating never-ending value.

-94-
Dying To Meet

On the Networking Rx podcast, guest Krister Ungerböck, a former global tech CEO and author of the book *22 Talk Shifts* shared about an encounter on the final mile of his first ultra-triathlon.

A fellow participant asked him, "If someone told you two years ago that you'd have become this person, what would say?" Ungerböck answered, "I'd say that I can't wait to meet my future self." The fellow participant responded, "Do you know what happens when you become the person you're dying to meet? Other people are dying to meet you too."

Who do you aspire to be? If it's merely someone ho-hum, then you can't expect that others will be eager to become part of your world. But if you work towards a vision of yourself that amazes you, you will draw into your life legions of people. And these people will surround you with appreciation and support.

The lesson: Aspire to become someone others are dying to meet.

-95-
Light Up a Room

Others tend to mimic what you do. If you're in a conversation and you lean forward, the other person will likely lean forward too. Cross your arms. In time, they will follow that lead. Smile. People will smile back. Laugh and they chuckle too.

Science is just starting to understand how this all works. But you don't need a clear understanding, do you? You just need to know that it works and put it into action.

How? When you walk into a meeting or gathering, you don't have to settle for merely gauging the vibe of the room. Rather, you can positively impact the mood through you own demeanor.

You can infuse it with confidence by carrying yourself with a degree of poise. You can bring happiness with your simile and playful laugh. You can introduce a sense of generosity by being interested in the well-being of others. In short, your presence can serve to light up the room.

-96-
Riddled With Forgiveness

Human beings are the most diverse creatures on the planet. No two are alike. Despite this diversity, there is one thing that all humans have in common. None are perfect and, as such, each and every one of us makes mistakes.

While some are ghastlier than others, everyone makes mistakes. Some are accidental. Regrettably, others are deliberate. Whatever the case, remember that everyone makes mistakes. It is part of being human.

Knowing that, you should endeavor to become more tolerate and forgiving when someone commits a blunder. No one says this is easy. In fact, at times it can be hard, especially when it impacts you.

But you need to remember you make mistakes too. And just as you hope that people will grace you with tolerance, understanding, and an opportunity for a reasonable explanation, that's all others want, too. So, yes, life is riddled with mistakes. You can counterbalance that by leading a life that is riddled with forgiveness.

-97-
Life Prepares You For Life

In her book *The Light in 9/11: Shocked By Kindness; Healed By Love*, professional speaker and enlightened living coach Lisa Luckett shared this insight: "Life prepares you for life."

Think about it. Every moment in life serves to prepare you for the next moment in life. You learned to count, right? And that set you up perfectly to understand addition and subtraction. Learning your ABC's paved the way for learning to read and write.

But beyond "reading, writing and arithmetic," the notion of "life prepares you for life" extends to your entire world. You will get through the challenges and issues of today because you have the experiences of all the days that came before.

So, as Luckett implies, don't be afraid of tomorrow. Don't be apprehensive of the unknown. You are well situated to take on whatever comes your way. In short, you've got this. Never forget that your life has prepared you for the life ahead.

-98-
Less Energy Relationships

When people mention the term networking, it often conjures images of suiting up in business attire, grabbing a handful of business cards and driving off to a Chamber event or other business gathering to rub elbows with strangers.

That's good. Much of building a solid network involves striking up conversations and building relationships with people you really don't know. But what about the legions of people that were once an active part of your network but have drifted away.

These are the people who might have moved to another part of town. Or who took a new position outside of your usual circles. Or perhaps marriage and children have made them (or you) less available.

Whatever the case, focus on reconnecting with these people, rather than devoting the lion's share of your time to meeting new people. Why? These people already know, like and trust you. Thus, it takes less energy to make the relationship productive.

-99-
Save Your World

Eons ago, circling a distant star were two planets - Givitas and Pridious - similar in every way, except one. The citizen of Givitas freely asked for help when needed and got it. As a result, they were eager to share with others.

On Pridious, however, people were too proud to seek help. And thus didn't get anything from others. In time, they morphed into resentful people, who were not interested in sharing at all.

One day, a massive cosmic storm was bearing down on this two-planet solar system. The people of Givitas ensured the safety of all by cooperatively seeking answers and sharing help to formulate a defense.

Pridious had all the same resources and knowledge. However, without the humility to seek help or the interest in sharing, they lacked the capacity to collectively craft an appropriate protection. As such, sadly, the planet was forever lost in the storm.

Save your world. Don't be too proud to ask. Don't become too selfish to share.

-100-
The Networking Rainbow

Do you want to know the difference between networking and selling? It's simple.

In sales, you identify a prospect. Pursue them diligently. Convince them to buy from you. They pay. You deliver. Transaction over.

Networking, on the other hand, is best summed up in Rob Thomas' book *Who Do You Need To Meet?* In it, Thomas shares, "Networking is about getting to know the other person, finding commonalities, synergy and then nurturing the relationship for the long term. It's about becoming valuable to others, so that when the time comes, they will remember you."

Thomas refers to the "remember you," as the gold at the end of the networking rainbow. And he reminds us that this rainbow keeps paying off, again and again.

Think about it. As you interact with new and existing contacts, are you simply looking to rain pitches on them relative to the goods and services you offer? Or are you serving others and building the networking rainbow in your world?

-101-
CLAIM Others; Build A Community

Dea Irby, published author and TEDx speaker, understands the value of belonging. Over decades of living in over 15 different homes across five southern states building churches with her husband, she's come to realize that people long for you to CLAIM them. To Irby, CLAIM is simply an acronym.

The C stands for *Chosen*. People need to feel as if you've selected them to be in your life.

The L stands for *Loved*. Likewise, people need to feel that you care about them deeply.

The A ... *Acknowledged*. People also need you to recognize them for their contribution.

The I ... *Invested* In. People need to know that you're willing to devote time and energy to them.

And, finally, the M stands for *Matter*. People need to believe that they matter to the cause.

Chosen. Loved. Acknowledged. Invested In. And matter. As Irby implies, if you CLAIM others, you will effectively build a community.

There you have it—101 essays. But we wanted to offer a bonus essay. Before we do, if you're interested in exploring other books, content, and programs by Frank Agin, visit frankagin.com or simply search "Frank Agin" on whatever platform you use to get great content.

-102-
Be Crystal Clear

No doubt, you network for things. Referrals. Introductions. Information. Opportunities. In general, you're looking to achieve success.

Now, a key to success at ... well ... really anything is being clear as to what you want. That is you need to have a vivid picture in your mind as to where you want to be. And you need to have a sense as to what you need to get there.

And this is true of networking too. You see, if you don't know what you want (in terms of referrals, introductions, information, and opportunities) then you don't know what you're looking for. And, if you don't know what looking for, then you can't articulate it. And if you can't do that, then you can't enlist the help of others to find it.

So, take the time to get crystal clear on what you want and what you're looking for.

About The Author

Frank Agin is president of AmSpirit Business Connections, which empowers entrepreneurs, sales representatives, and professionals to become successful and gain more referrals through networking.

He also shares information and insights on professional relationships, business networking and best practices for generating referrals on his Networking Rx podcast and through various professional programs.

Finally, Frank is the author of several books, including *Foundational Networking: Building Know, Like & Trust to Create a Life of Extraordinary Success*. See all his books and programs at frankagin.com. You can reach him at frankagin@amspirit.com.